W9-CVO-380

ISBN 978-1-934655-24-5

P.O. Box 262550 • Baton Rouge, Louisiana 70826-2550
Website: www.jsm.org • Email: info@jsm.org
225-768-7000

TABLE OF CONTENTS

CHAPTER **PAGE**

Spiritual Adultery

The Cross Of Christ Series

Introduction

THE CROSS OF CHRIST, SPIRITUAL ADULTERY

INTRODUCTION

On a Sunday Morning in October of 2005, I was ministering at Family Worship Center. The Spirit of the Lord moved mightily that morning. In fact, we aired the Service over Television a few weeks later.

I was dealing with the subject of *"demon possession"* and *"demon oppression."* I was instructing the people on the falseness of the teaching, as believed by some, that a Born-Again Believer can be demon possessed (i.e., at the same time as *"born-again"*). But yet, as I went on to explain to them, Believers most definitely can be oppressed by demon spirits.

The word *"oppressed"* in the Greek is *"katadunasteuo,"* which means *"to exercise dominion against"* or *"to have dominion over."* Without any fear of contradiction, I believe one could say that every single Believer who has ever lived has, at one time or the other, experienced *"demon oppression."*

The Scripture says:

"How God anointed Jesus of Nazareth with the Holy Spirit and with Power: Who went about doing good, and healing all who were oppressed of the Devil; for God was with Him" (Acts 10:38).

Demon possession comes from within, while demon oppression comes from without. Demon oppression takes the form of emotional disturbance, fear, depression, and some forms of physical illnesses.

VICTORY

I was describing to the people this problem, how that in years past I had experienced it myself, even to such an extent as to be unbearable. And then while I was preaching, even explaining these very things, all of a sudden it dawned on me that I had not experienced any type of demonic oppression since the Lord began in 1997 to open up to my heart the Message of the Cross.

I related that to the people, and did so with great joy. After the Service, I thought about it very carefully and tried to recollect if I had actually forgotten some particular periods of time since 1997. There were no times that came to my mind then, and no times at the present. In other words, by the Grace of God, and according to what Christ has done for us at the Cross, and my Faith in that Finished Work, I have not experienced one single moment of demonic oppression during these years.

And then teaching over our Daily Telecast, *"A Study In The Word,"* and dealing with this very subject, it came to me that not only have I not suffered any type of demonic oppression during this period of time (since 1997), but there has never been even one hour of discouragement. I realize that's quite a statement, but I know it to be true.

Yes, we have faced all type of problems at the Ministry (which I will not bother to enumerate here) which have caused us much concern. But I always knew that the Lord would handle the situation, which He always has.

BEFORE THE CROSS

Before the Lord began to open up to me the great Message of the Cross, I experienced discouragement and demonic oppression more times than I care to remember. At times, it was to such an extent that it almost destroyed me. But the Cross of Christ, which speaks of my understanding of what Jesus there did, has changed everything.

It is sad, but most modern Believers are trying to live their Christian experience by trying to mix the *"Old Covenant"* with the *"New Covenant."* They little take advantage of what Jesus has done for them at the Cross, mostly because they don't understand what our Lord did at the Cross. Every single true Believer in the world has *"more abundant life"* (Jn. 10:10), but only a precious few Believers are enjoying that *"more abundant life."* They are not enjoying it and not experiencing its fullness simply because they do not understand the Cross.

That's the reason that the false teaching of Believers being demon-possessed has such an audience. Believers are plagued by certain types of sin and they struggle unsuccessfully to overcome them; so when a Preacher tells them that their problem is a demon spirit, that they are possessed by a particular demon, they believe it to be true. However, it isn't true!

YOU SHALL KNOW THE TRUTH AND THE TRUTH SHALL MAKE YOU FREE

This is the problem: Modern Believers do not know the Truth of the Gospel. They have some understanding, but not very much.

Jesus said: *"And you shall know the Truth, and the Truth shall make you free"* (Jn. 8:32).

The modern Church does not know the Truth of the Gospel, and that's the problem of the modern Church! That means it doesn't understand what the New Covenant is all about.

The New Covenant is the meaning of the Cross, and the Cross is the meaning of the New Covenant. What Jesus did at the Cross atoned for all sin, past, present, and future, at least for all who will believe (Jn. 3:16), thereby making it possible for man to be redeemed.

THE CROSS OF CHRIST IS THE FOUNDATION OF REDEMPTION

The Cross of Christ actually is the Foundation principle on which the entirety of the fabric of the Gospel is built. It was conceived in the mind of the Godhead even before the foundation of the world.

Peter said, and I quote from THE EXPOSITOR'S STUDY BIBLE:

"Forasmuch as you know that you were not redeemed with corruptible things, as silver and gold (presents the fact that the most precious commodities [silver and gold] could not redeem fallen man), *from your vain conversation* (vain lifestyle) *received by tradition from your fathers* (speaks of original sin that is passed on from father to child at conception)*;*

"But with the Precious Blood of Christ (presents the payment, which proclaims the poured out Life of Christ on behalf of sinners), *as of a Lamb without blemish and without spot* (speaks of the lambs offered as substitutes in the Old Jewish economy; the Death of Christ was not an execution or assassination, but rather a Sacrifice; the Offering of Himself presented a Perfect Sacrifice, for He was Perfect in every respect [Ex. 12:5])*:*

"Who verily was foreordained before the foundation of the world (refers to the fact that God, in His Omniscience, knew He would create man, man would fall, and man would be redeemed by Christ going to the Cross; this was all done before the Universe was created; this means the Cross of Christ is the Foundation

Doctrine of all Doctrine, referring to the fact that all Doctrine must be built upon that Foundation, or else it is specious), *but was manifest in these last times for you* (refers to the invisible God Who, in the Person of the Son, was made visible to human eyesight by assuming a human body and human limitations)" (I Pet. 1:18-20).

All of this tells us that even before God created man, He knew, through foreknowledge, that man would fall; therefore, the Godhead determined that man would be redeemed by God becoming man and going to the Cross, which would be the offering up of Himself as a Perfect Sacrifice, which alone would satisfy the demands of a thrice-Holy God.

So we learn from this that the Cross of Christ, determined before the foundation of the world, is the Foundation upon which the Redemption Plan is built. This means that any doctrine that is not based squarely on the Foundation of the Cross of Christ will, in some way, prove to be false. One might say that all false doctrine begins by an improper understanding of the Cross, or else by gross unbelief in the Cross.

SPIRITUAL ADULTERY

All of this means that every single way fomented by man, which means every way not originated by the Lord, which refers to every way not based on the Cross, is *"spiritual adultery."* As important as this subject is, most Christians have never even heard the term, much less understand what it means.

As stated, it refers to any effort to live for God by any means other than Faith in Christ and what Christ has done for us at the Cross. Such a position, even as we will study in this Study Guide, is *"spiritual adultery."* It should be obvious that such a direction is extremely detrimental as it regards Spiritual Growth because, basically, it will hinder, if not altogether stop, all Spiritual Growth. But regrettably that's the condition of virtually the entirety of the modern Church. It is living in a state of *"spiritual adultery"* simply because it does not understand the Cross, or else it doesn't believe in what Jesus there did.

To be frank, the greatest problem of all is not ignorance, but rather unbelief, a subject which we will deal with more directly in this Volume.

Chapter 1

Spiritual Adultery In The Old Testament

CHAPTER ONE

SELF-HELP STUDY NOTES

SPIRITUAL ADULTERY IN THE OLD TESTAMENT

It is through the Apostle Paul that the Holy Spirit gave the principle of *"spiritual adultery,"* which he deals with in the first four Verses of the Seventh Chapter of Romans, which we will address in the next Chapter. However, Paul derived this concept from the Lord's dealings with His people in the Old Testament.

The Scripture says, *"Moreover he* (Jehoram) *made high places in the mountains of Judah and caused the inhabitants of Jerusalem to commit fornication and compelled Judah thereto"* (II Chron. 21:11).

Concerning Judah, the Holy Spirit through the Prophet Ezekiel said, *"You have also committed fornication with the Egyptians your neighbors, great of flesh; and have increased your whoredoms, to provoke Me to anger"* (Ezek. 16:26, 29).

The Holy Spirit through the Prophet Jeremiah also said,

"And I saw, when for all the causes whereby backsliding Israel committed adultery I had put her away, and given her a bill of divorce; yet her treacherous sister Judah feared not, but went and played the harlot also.

"And it came to pass through the lightness of her whoredom that she defiled the land, and committed adultery with stones and with stocks" (Jer. 3:8-9).

Most of the time in the Old Testament when the Scripture speaks of adultery and fornication, it is speaking of idolatry. In other words, the Lord looked at Himself as Israel's husband. He said through the Prophet Isaiah:

"For your Maker is your Husband; the LORD of Hosts is His Name; and your Redeemer the Holy One of Israel; the God of the whole Earth shall He be called" (Isa. 54:5).

Back in Jeremiah 3:8, the Holy Spirit plainly says through the Prophet that the Lord divorced Israel because of her idolatry.

"And I saw, when for all the causes whereby backsliding Israel committed adultery I had put her away, and given her a bill of divorce" (Jer. 3:8).

The Lord, as Israel's Husband, demanded faithfulness to Him, as should be obvious. So when Israel went into idolatry, in the Mind of God, Israel was committing adultery or fornication against Him, which means that she was being grossly unfaithful to Him. After warning her time and time again, through Prophet after Prophet, finally there was no choice but for God to divorce Israel, which He did.

THE MARRIAGE BOND BETWEEN HUSBAND AND WIFE

Our Lord used the same principle regarding the marriage bond between husband and wife, as it regards divorce and remarriage. It has the same reference as it did between God and Israel of old.

The Lord said, and I quote from THE EXPOSITOR'S STUDY BIBLE:

"And I say unto you, Whosoever shall put away his wife, except it be for fornication (an adulterous lifestyle) *and shall marry another, commits adultery: and whoso marries her which is put away does commit adultery* (if the marriage is dissolved for Scriptural grounds — fornication or desertion [I Cor. 7:15], remarriage is Scripturally allowed)" (Mat. 19:9).

If fornication (an adulterous lifestyle) is the manner of either husband or wife, such a marriage can remain such in name only, as would be obvious. And if such a marriage is dissolved because one party engages such a lifestyle, the innocent party, whether husband or wife, is free to marry again.

When the Lord divorced Israel, which He was forced to do because of their fornication (idolatrous lifestyle), He then married, one might say, the Church.

Paul said, *"For I am jealous over you with Godly jealousy* (refers to the *'jealousy of God'* (Ex. 20:5; 34:14; Nah. 1:2): *for I have espoused you to one husband* (not jealous at the Corinthians' affection for himself, but for their affection for Christ), *that I may present you as a chaste virgin to Christ* (they must not commit spiritual adultery, which refers to trusting in things other than Christ and the Cross)" (II Cor. 11:2).

THE BOOK OF REVELATION

Old Testament terminology is used in the Book of Revelation, despite the fact that it is in the New Testament.

As John the Beloved saw this great Vision, he said, and I quote from THE EXPOSITOR'S STUDY BIBLE:

"And there came one of the seven Angels which had the seven vials, and talked with me (probably is the seventh Angel; however, we actually have no way of truly knowing), *saying unto me, Come hither; I*

will show unto you the judgment of the great whore who sits upon many waters (the *'great whore'* refers to all the religions of the world that have ever been, which are devised by men as a substitute for *'Jesus Christ and Him Crucified'*; God's Way is Christ and Him Crucified Alone; as well, the *'many waters'* are a symbol for multitudes of people [Vs. 15]):

"With whom (the great whore, i.e., all type of religions) *the kings of the Earth* (from the very beginning, most nations have been ruled by some type of religion) *have committed fornication* (all religions devised by men, and even the parts of Christianity that have been corrupted, are labeled by the Lord as *'spiritual fornication'* [Rom. 7:1-4]), *and the inhabitants of the Earth have been made drunk with the wine of her fornication* (proclaims the addiction of religion; the doing of religion is the most powerful narcotic there is)" (Rev. 17:1-2).

Again I wish to emphasize the point that the Holy Spirit here labels every way supposedly of God that is not *"Jesus Christ and Him Crucified"* as a wrong way, a false way, i.e., *"spiritual fornication."* The Lord has provided His great Redemption Plan for lost humanity. It was done even from before the foundation of the world (I Pet. 1:18-20). God would become Man in order to go to the Cross, for this is the only way that a Perfect Sacrifice could be provided. We fallen sons of Adam's lost race had no way to save ourselves.

So if man was to be saved, God would have to initiate the process from its very beginning. Polluted, corrupted, fallen man could not devise anything that God could accept. But that's the problem with the world, and that has always been the problem with the world. The unredeemed attempt to manufacture another god other than Jehovah, while the Church attempts to manufacture another sacrifice other than Jesus Christ and Him Crucified.

SELF-HELP STUDY NOTES

Chapter 2

The Illustration Of The Marriage Bond

CHAPTER TWO

SELF-HELP
STUDY NOTES

THE ILLUSTRATION OF THE MARRIAGE BOND

When the Lord desired to illustrate the relationship that every Believer should have with Christ, He used the marriage bond to do so. It is given to us in the first four verses of Romans, Chapter 7.

I'll quote from THE EXPOSITOR'S STUDY BIBLE, giving the entirety of the Passage and the expository notes.

"Know ye not, Brethren (Paul is speaking to Believers), *(for I speak to them who know the Law,)* (he is speaking of the Law of Moses, but it could refer to any type of religious Law) *how that the Law has dominion over a man as long as he lives?* (The Law has dominion as long as he tries to live by Law. Regrettably, not understanding the Cross regarding Sanctification, virtually the entirety of the Church is presently trying to live for God by means of the Law. Let the Believer understand that there are only two places he can be, Grace or Law. If he doesn't understand the Cross as it refers to Sanctification, which is the only means of victory, he will automatically be under Law, which guarantees failure.)

"For the woman which has an husband is bound by the Law to her husband so long as he lives (presents Paul using the analogy of the marriage bond)*; but if the husband be dead, she is loosed from the Law of her husband* (meaning that she is free to marry again).

"So then if, while her husband lives, she be married to another man, she shall be called an adulteress (in effect, the woman now has two husbands, at least in the eyes of God; following this analogy, the Holy Spirit through Paul will give us a great truth; many Christians are living a life of spiritual adultery; they are married to Christ, but they are, in effect, serving another husband, *"the Law"*; it is quite an analogy!)*: but if her husband be dead* (the Law is dead by virtue of Christ having fulfilled the Law in every respect), *she is free from that Law* (if the husband dies, the woman is free to marry and serve another; the Law of Moses, being satisfied in Christ, is now dead to the Believer and the Believer is free to serve Christ without the Law having any part or parcel in his life or living)*; so that she is no adulteress, though she be married to another man* (presents the Believer as now married to Christ, and no longer under obligation to the Law).

"Wherefore, my Brethren, you also are become dead to the Law (the Law is not dead per se, but we are dead to the Law because we are

dead to its effects; this means that we are not to try to live for God by means of *"Law,"* whether the Law of Moses, or Laws made up by other men or of ourselves; we are to be dead to all Law) *by the Body of Christ* (this refers to the Crucifixion of Christ, which satisfied the demands of the broken Law we could not satisfy; but Christ did it for us; having fulfilled the Law in every respect, the Christian is not obligated to Law in any fashion, only to Christ and what He did at the Cross)*; that you should be married to another* (speaking of Christ), *even to Him Who is raised from the dead* (we are raised with Him in newness of life, and we should ever understand that Christ has met, does meet, and shall meet our every need; we look to Him exclusively, referring to what He did for us at the Cross), *that we should bring forth fruit unto God* (proper fruit can only be brought forth by the Believer constantly looking to the Cross; in fact, Christ must never be separated from the Work of the Cross; to do so is to produce *'another Jesus'* [II Cor. 11:4])*"* (Rom. 7:1-4).

SPIRITUAL ADULTERY

The Message given here by Paul is clear. As we have already stated, the Holy Spirit through Him uses the marriage bond as an illustration. The wife is to be faithful to her husband. If she is unfaithful to her husband by cohabiting with another man, the Holy Spirit through Paul plainly states, *"She shall be called an adulteress"* (7:3).

Paul is using this as an analogy, an illustration, if you will, to explain the marriage bond between the Believer and Christ. Clearly and plainly, the Holy Spirit through the Apostle says that we Believers are *"married to another, even to Him Who is raised from the dead,"* speaking, of course, of Christ (7:4).

FAITHFUL TO CHRIST

We as Believers are to be one hundred percent faithful to Christ.

Now most Believers would argue that they are doing exactly that, being faithful to Christ. But one can truly be faithful to Christ only by totally and completely trusting Him and what He has done for us at the Cross. In fact, our trust in Christ and the Cross must be without limit. In other words, the Cross of Christ must ever be the Object of our Faith. If our faith is transferred to something else, the Lord will look at us as a *"spiritual adulterer."* In other words, we are not being faithful to Christ.

The key to all of this is our understanding that every single thing that we receive from the Lord comes to us exclusively from Christ as the Source and the Cross as the Means. If our faith is in anything else, and it doesn't matter how good the other thing might be, we are actually living in a state of *"spiritual adultery."*

Let me say that again:

All of this means that we are being unfaithful to Christ.

SELF-HELP STUDY NOTES

ANOTHER JESUS, ANOTHER SPIRIT, ANOTHER GOSPEL

In dealing with this problem in a slightly different manner, the Apostle Paul warns the Corinthians about this very same thing. I am going to quote four verses from THE EXPOSITOR'S STUDY BIBLE. They are:

"Would to God you could bear with me a little in my folly: and indeed bear with me. (In effect, the Apostle is saying, *'Indulge me.'*)

"For I am jealous over you with Godly jealousy (refers to the *'jealousy of God'* [Ex. 20:5; 34:14; Nah. 1:2])*: for I have espoused you to one husband* (not jealous of the Corinthians' affection for himself, but of their affection for Christ)*, that I may present you as a chaste virgin to Christ.* (They must not commit spiritual adultery, which refers to trusting in things other than Christ and the Cross.)

"But I fear, lest by any means, as the serpent beguiled Eve through his subtilty (the strategy of Satan)*, so your minds should be corrupted from the simplicity that is in Christ.* (The Gospel of Christ is simple, but men complicate it by adding to the Message.)

"For if he who comes preaching another Jesus (a Jesus who is not of the Cross)*, whom we have not preached* (Paul's Message was *'Jesus Christ and Him Crucified'*; anything else is *'another Jesus'*)*, or if you receive another spirit* (which is produced by preaching another Jesus)*, which you have not received* (that's not what you received when we preached the True Gospel to you)*, or another Gospel, which you have not accepted* (anything other than *'Jesus Christ and Him Crucified'* is *'another gospel'*)*, you might well bear with him.* (The Apostle is telling the Corinthians they have, in fact, sinned because they tolerated these false apostles who had come in, bringing *'another gospel,'* which was something other than Christ and the Cross)" (II Cor. 11:1-4).

WHAT IS PAUL TALKING ABOUT WHEN HE REFERS TO *"ANOTHER JESUS"*?

Tragically, that's where most of the modern Church is presently. It is serving and trusting in *"another Jesus,"* which was produced by *"another spirit."* This means it is not the Holy Spirit, Who presents *"another gospel,"* which the Apostle also stated there *"is not another."*

Let me quote again from THE EXPOSITOR'S STUDY BIBLE.

The Apostle says the following to the Galatians:

"I marvel that you are so soon removed from Him (the Holy Spirit) *Who called you into the Grace of Christ* (made possible by the Cross) *unto another Gospel* (anything which doesn't have the Cross as its Object of Faith)*:*

"Which is not another (presents the fact that Satan's aim is not so much to deny the Gospel, which he can little do, as to corrupt it)*; but there be some who trouble you, and would pervert the Gospel of Christ* (once again, to make the object of faith something other than the Cross*"* (Gal. 1:6-7).

"Another Jesus," which presents *"another gospel,"* is, as stated, the bane of the modern Church.

Let's say it another way.

If our faith is not exclusively in Christ and the Cross, then, pure and simple, we are not serving the Christ of the Bible, but rather *"another Jesus."* If Jesus is divorced in any manner from the Cross, separated in any way, then it's *"another Jesus,"* which is the same thing as saying *"spiritual adultery"* in another way.

JESUS CHRIST IS THE SOURCE AND THE CROSS IS THE MEANS

What do we mean by that heading?

Actually, the statement is simple. It means that the *"Source"* of everything we receive from God is the Lord Jesus Christ, and the *"Means"* by which He gives these things to us, whatever they might be, is the Cross. This shoots down every other means of Sanctification such as *"The Purpose Driven Life,"* or *"The Government of Twelve,"* or *"The Word of Faith,"* or *"Denominationalism,"* or a hundred and one other things that could be named. All of these particular methods are devised by men, which means they were not originated by the Holy Spirit, which means they are not Scriptural. They should be shunned at all costs!

Every Chapter in the Bible, from Genesis 1:1 through Revelation 22:21, points in some way to Christ, and, above all, what He did for us at the Cross.

CAIN AND ABEL

The Fourth Chapter of Genesis presents to us the saga of the offspring of the First Family. We speak of Cain and Abel. Despite the Fall of the First Family, the Lord had told them how they could have communion with Him and forgiveness of sins. It would be through the sacrifice of an innocent victim, namely a lamb. It was explained in detail to Adam and Eve, with evidence that they heeded the Word, at least for a period of time.

I'm going to quote from George Williams, regarding his comments as given in the Student's Commentary. He said:

"Eve is mentioned four times in the Bible (Gen. 3:20; 4:1; II Cor. 11:3; I Tim. 2:13). *She names her sons 'Cain,' meaning 'that is begotten,' and 'Abel,' meaning 'that is vanity,' thus illustrating the ignorance into which she had plunged because she had trusted Satan for knowledge.*

"At Cain's birth, she joyfully cries, 'I have gotten the man promised by Jehovah!' Very soon she learns that he was out of the Evil One (I Jn. 3:12), *and when his brother is given to her, she exclaims with anguish, 'Vanity!'*

"The brothers dress their altars at the 'door' of the mysterious Tabernacle in which God dwelt, and attached to which is the flaming sword. There is no difference between the brothers, but an eternal difference between their Sacrifices. They are both corrupt branches of a decayed tree, both born outside Eden, and both guilty, both sinners, no moral difference, and both sentenced to death. The words 'by faith' (Heb. 11:4) *teach that God had revealed a way of approach to Him* (Rom. 10:17). *Abel accepts this Way, Cain rejects it. Abel's Altar speaks of Repentance, of Faith, and of the Precious Blood of Christ, the Lamb of God without blemish. Cain's altar tells of pride, unbelief, and self-righteousness.*

"Abel's altar is beautiful to God's eye and repulsive to man's. Cain's altar is beautiful to man's eye and repulsive to God's. These 'altars' exist today. Around the one, that is, Christ and His Atoning Work, few are gathered; around the other, many. God accepts the slain lamb and rejects the offered fruit; and the offering being rejected, so, of necessity, is the offeror."

IF THE SACRIFICE IS ACCEPTED, THE ONE OFFERING THE SACRIFICE IS ACCEPTED

The Lord looked very little at Cain or Abel. It was obvious as to what both of them were — desperate sinners in need of a Saviour.

Let us state that again:

Man's need is a Saviour and not a problem solver, and that Saviour is none other than the Lord Jesus Christ. Salvation is afforded by Him through what He did for us at the Cross.

It is the Sacrifice which is the all-important principle in this Salvation

SELF-HELP STUDY NOTES

Plan. As stated, the Lord already knows what man is. Man is hopelessly lost and unable to save himself, which means the die is cast. So the all-important aspect of this great Salvation Plan is the Sacrifice. If the Sacrifice is acceptable to God, then the one who offers the Sacrifice is instantly acceptable also.

Before the Cross, it was a lamb, which was an innocent victim, and which served as a Substitute until Christ would come. While it was woefully insufficient to *"take away sins,"* it nevertheless served as a stopgap measure, so to speak, until the Reality would come (Heb. 10:4).

Therefore, the Sacrifice being all-important, God would not accept the Sacrifice offered by Cain, which was the fruit of his own hands. He did accept the Sacrifice offered by Abel; the Sacrifice being accepted, Abel was accepted also. It is the same presently!

If our faith presently is in Christ and what He did for us at the Cross, we are instantly accepted (Ex. 12:13; Rom. 5:1-2; 6:1-14; I Cor. 1:17-18, 21, 23; 2:2; Gal., Chpt. 5; 6:14, etc.) But man's problem is, and always has been, that he attempts to substitute another sacrifice other than the Cross. When this is done, *"spiritual adultery"* is the result.

LET HIM BE ACCURSED

This is so important, so significant, so absolute, so necessary, that the Holy Spirit through the Apostle Paul said, and again I quote from THE EXPOSITOR'S STUDY BIBLE:

"But though we (Paul and his associates)*, or an Angel from Heaven, preach any other gospel unto you than that which we have preached unto you* (Jesus Christ and Him Crucified)*, let him be accursed* (eternally condemned); the Holy Spirit speaks this through Paul, making this very serious).

"As we said before, so say I now again (at some time past, he had said the same thing to them, making their defection even more serious)*, If any man preach any other gospel unto you* (anything other than the Cross) *than that you have received* (which saved your souls)*, let him be accursed* (*'eternally condemned,'* which means the loss of the soul)" (Gal. 1:8-9).

This destroys the fallacious doctrine that there are many ways to God.

Please note the following:

1. Jesus Christ is the only way to God (Jn. 14:6).
2. The only way to Jesus Christ is through the Cross (Lk. 9:23).
3. The only way to the Cross is a denial of self (Lk. 9:23).

Let us quote the Words of Christ, and do so from THE EXPOSITOR'S STUDY BIBLE:

"And He said to them all, If any man will come after Me (the criteria for Discipleship)*, let him deny himself* (not asceticism, as many think, but rather that one denies one's own willpower, self-will, strength, and ability, depending totally on Christ)*, and take up his Cross* (the benefits of the Cross, looking exclusively to what Jesus did there to meet our every need) *daily* (this is so important, our looking to the Cross, that we must renew our faith in what Christ has done for us, even on a daily basis, for Satan will ever try to move us away from the Cross as the object of our faith, which always spells disaster)*, and follow Me* (Christ can be followed only by the Believer looking to the Cross, understanding what it accomplished, and by that means alone [I Cor. 1:17-18, 21, 23; 2:2; Eph. 2:13-18; Col. 2:14-15)*"* (Lk. 9:23).

So, we are told clearly and plainly in the Word of God that the only gospel that the Lord will recognize is the Gospel of *"Jesus Christ and Him Crucified."* Anything else constitutes *"spiritual adultery,"* which the Lord cannot bless, as should be overly obvious.

SELF-HELP STUDY NOTES

Chapter 3

The Cross Of Christ And Sanctification

CHAPTER THREE

SELF-HELP STUDY NOTES

THE CROSS OF CHRIST AND SANCTIFICATION

Most Christians have a modicum of knowledge concerning the Cross in connection with Salvation; however, most have almost no knowledge whatsoever regarding the Cross and Sanctification. Strangely enough, the Apostle Paul, to whom the meaning of the New Covenant was given (which is the meaning of the Cross [Gal. 1:11-12]), addresses a large part of his Epistles almost exclusively to the Cross of Christ as it refers to Sanctification. This should tell us just how important this subject is. There is actually nothing more important to the Child of God than how to live for God, which is what the Sanctification process is all about.

Whether they understand it or not, almost every manner, way, scheme, and idea presented by Preachers involves the Sanctification process. The great exception to this would be the Word of Faith Doctrine, which almost exclusively addresses itself to the idea of getting rich, which is grossly unbiblical, but which, due to the greed which seems to reside in most every human heart, has a mass appeal.

When it comes to *"The Purpose Driven Life"* and *"The Government of Twelve"* doctrines, and a hundred and one others that could be named, all of these involve the Sanctification process, and all are man-devised, which means they simply will not work. The end result actually will be the very opposite of a victorious life; the end result will be destruction.

THE HOLY SPIRIT AND SANCTIFICATION

The Sanctification process is a Work of the Holy Spirit and of Him Alone. This means that whatever needs to be done in our lives, the Holy Spirit Alone can carry out the process. And, to be sure, there is much that needs to be done. There is no way that all the efforts, schemes, or plans of man can effect this of which we speak (Rom. 8:11).

In other words, Christlikeness, Holiness, the Fruit of the Spirit, and other desirable characteristics in the Child of God can only be brought about by the Holy Spirit. God views anything else as a fake!

So the great question is, *"How does the Holy Spirit carry out the Sanctification process?"*

Here I will give a brief summary, but I encourage the Reader to obtain our Study Guide on this subject: THE CROSS OF CHRIST, HOW

SELF-HELP STUDY NOTES

THE HOLY SPIRIT WORKS.

We are told exactly how the Spirit of God works in a number of Passages, but the most telling is the following, and I continue to quote from THE EXPOSITOR'S STUDY BIBLE:

"For the Law (that which we are about to give is a Law of God, devised by the Godhead in eternity past [I Pet. 1:18-20]; this Law, in fact, is *'God's Prescribed Order of Victory') of the Spirit* (Holy Spirit, i.e., *'The Way the Spirit works') of Life* (all life comes from Christ, but through the Holy Spirit [Jn. 16:13-14]) *in Christ Jesus* (any time Paul uses this term or one of its derivatives, he is, without fail, referring to what Christ did at the Cross, which makes this *'life'* possible) *has made me free* (given me total Victory) *from the Law of sin and death* (these are the two most powerful Laws in the Universe; the *'Law of the Spirit of Life in Christ Jesus'* alone is stronger than the *'Law of sin and death'*; this means that if the Believer attempts to live for God by any manner other than Faith in Christ and the Cross, he is doomed to failure)" (Rom. 8:2).

As stated, in this Passage we are told exactly how the Holy Spirit works. Totally and completely, He works within the parameters of the Finished Work of Christ, i.e., *"the Cross."* In fact, He will not work outside of the Cross, not in any capacity.

The Holy Spirit will most definitely remain with the Believer even though the Believer might be functioning in a state of *"spiritual adultery"*; however, under such circumstances, He is greatly limited, as should be obvious. To be frank, the Holy Spirit doesn't demand much of us, but He does demand that our faith be exclusively in Christ and the Cross, and that means that nothing else must be added. If anything else is added, it cancels out the Cross and becomes *"spiritual adultery."*

Once again, coming into play are the marriage vows which Paul used in the first four verses of the Seventh Chapter of Romans. If the woman is unfaithful to her husband, *"she shall be called an adulteress."* Paul then tells us plainly that we are married to Christ. As such, He is to supply our every need, whatever it might be, which He does solely by and through the Cross. As we've previously stated, this demands that the Cross must ever be the Object of our Faith.

If our faith is correct, the Holy Spirit, Who Alone can bring to pass in our lives that which is needed, will work mightily on our behalf. He will then begin to develop His Fruit, to develop Righteousness and Holiness, and to make us what we ought to be.

Chapter 4

Fight The Good Fight Of Faith

CHAPTER FOUR

SELF-HELP STUDY NOTES

FIGHT THE GOOD FIGHT OF FAITH

The whole matter is a question of faith; it never is a question of works. Works, of course, are important. But works must be the result of our faith and never the cause.

Works do not actually please God, even though they are important in their own way. It is Faith which pleases Him, and Faith alone!

Concerning this very thing, Paul said:

"For without Faith (in Christ and the Cross; any time Faith is mentioned, always and without exception, its root meaning is that its Object is Christ and the Cross; otherwise, it is faith God will not accept) *it is impossible to please Him* (faith in anything other than Christ and the Cross greatly displeases the Lord)*: for he who comes to God must believe that He is* (places Faith as the foundation and principle of the manner in which God deals with the human race), *and that He* (God) *is a rewarder of them who diligently seek Him* (seek Him on the premise of Christ and Him Crucified)*"* (Heb. 11:6).

Because it is so important, please allow us to say it again.

1. It is Faith alone which God recognizes.
2. It must, however, be Faith in Christ and the Cross (I Cor. 1:17-18, 23; 2:2; Gal., Chpt. 5; 6:14; Col. 2:14-15).
3. Having Faith in the Cross of Christ is the same as having Faith in the Word of God. In fact, the two are synonymous. The Story of the Bible in its entirety is the story of *"Jesus Christ and Him Crucified"* (Jn. 1:1, 14, 29).

THE FIGHT

I will continue to quote from THE EXPOSITOR'S STUDY BIBLE. Paul told Timothy:

"Fight the good fight of Faith (in essence, the only fight we're called upon to engage; every attack by Satan against the Believer, irrespective of its form, is to destroy or seriously weaken our Faith; he wants to push our Faith from the Cross to other things), *lay hold on Eternal Life* (we do such by understanding that all Life comes from Christ, and the Means is the Cross), *whereunto you are also called* (called to follow Christ) *and have professed a good profession before many witnesses*

(this does not refer to a particular occasion, but to the entirety of his life for Christ)" (I Tim. 6:12).

Just because the Believer has his Faith right, which refers to the Cross being its Object, and ever its Object, still, that doesn't mean that Satan is going to fold his tent, so to speak, and leave. Satan actually will do everything within his power to move one's Faith from Christ and the Cross to other things.

He doesn't care if your faith is in Christ and *"The Government of Twelve,"* or Christ and *"The Purpose Driven Life,"* or Christ and *"The Word of Faith,"* etc., because he knows that the Lord looks at such as *"another Jesus,"* etc. (II Cor. 11:4). He just doesn't want your faith to be exclusively in Christ and the Cross, and he will do everything within his power, mostly using Preachers, to move it elsewhere. This is where the *"fight"* comes in. And incidentally, it is a *"fight"* in which we must engage every single day.

That's why Jesus said that we must *"take up the Cross daily"* if we are to follow Him (Lk. 9:23).

However, even though it is a *"fight,"* still, it is a *"good fight,"* simply because it is the right fight.

THE RIGHT FIGHT

Tragically, most Christians are fighting battles that our Saviour has already fought and won a long, long time ago. He did it for us because we could not in any way have won such a fight.

Preachers preach long sermons on *"taking the land,"* when our Lord, in fact, took it at the Cross some 2,000 years ago. Preachers preach sermons on *"defeating the Jebusites, the Canaanites, etc.,"* when, in reality, our Lord defeated every power of darkness at the Cross. This means that we are trying to fight battles which already have been won, which, in truth, we could not win even if we fought them.

FIGHTING SIN

In the Word of God, we are not called upon to fight sin, per se, but rather to *"fight the good fight of Faith."* We fight sin in every capacity, and we must not fail to fight sin; but the problem of sin was addressed at the Cross by Christ, and He handled it in every capacity.

Yet, millions of Christians, even good Christians, spend most of their lives fighting sin in some way, and I speak of sin in their own lives. It is a battle that one cannot win. The battle has already been won.

Please note the following very carefully:

If we are fighting and winning, after a while we will fight and lose. Of that, one can be certain, no matter what type of fight it might be.

To be sure, sin is the problem as it regards the Christian, but there is one way to handle it, and only one way, and that is God's Prescribed Order of Victory.

What is that Prescribed Order of Victory?

For an extended coverage of this subject, please see our Study Guide: THE CROSS OF CHRIST, GOD'S PRESCRIBED ORDER OF VICTORY.

In brief, God's Prescribed Order of Victory is our Faith in Christ and what Christ did for us at the Cross. It is outlined perfectly in Romans, Chapter 6.

Whether they realize it or not, Christians who are spending their time fighting sin in their own lives are actually placing their faith in themselves. They may not think of it that way, but that's exactly what is happening. As a consequence, they are living in a state of *"spiritual adultery,"* which means that the Holy Spirit is not going to help them in this capacity. To be sure, the Holy Spirit is not going to help anyone remain in a state of spiritual adultery. He will help us get out of that state, but He will not help us while we are in that state.

Furthermore, whether we realize it or not, our efforts in this capacity constitute a gross insult to Christ. When we attempt to fight sin in our lives, we are stating that what Christ did at the Cross was not enough, so we have to add our efforts to what He already has done.

We might think pretty highly of ourselves and our efforts in combating the forces of darkness, but we truly are insulting Christ when we do this. As stated, this is a battle that the Believer cannot win, simply because it has already been won.

The only way to overcome sin is for the Believer to place his Faith exclusively in Christ and what Christ has done for us at the Cross. We must fight to hold our Faith in that position, and we continue to speak of the Cross. Then, to be sure, the Holy Spirit, Who is God and Who can do anything, will begin to greatly work on our behalf, thereby giving us the victory which He Alone can give.

Let me relate a little story that every Christian has heard at one time or another. I repeat it here simply because it illustrates the situation so perfectly. It also is a true story.

AN ILLUSTRATION

A young couple who lived in Ireland worked long and hard to save their money in order to buy a ticket from Ireland to the United States. In

SELF-HELP STUDY NOTES

other words, they wanted to emigrate to the Land of the Brave and the Home of the Free.

They finally saved enough money to purchase the least expensive ticket and were glad to get that.

Several days after they had left the harbor in Ireland, when they were actually not too far from America, one of the ship's pursers happened to pass by their tiny cabin. Being the most inexpensive fare, it was several decks below. When the purser saw that the cabin door was open and the man was standing close to the door, he stopped to chat for a few moments. He asked them, *"How has the trip been? Have you enjoyed it?"*

In the course of the conversation, he noticed a lot of cracker crumbs on the bed. Casually, the purser asked the couple, *"What are those?"*

The young wife patiently explained to him how hard and long they had worked to be able to save the money to buy the ticket to come to the United States. She continued that they only could afford the cheapest fare and that they had no money left over to buy food. As a result, she had packed a number of sandwiches and things of such nature for them to eat on the trip over.

Finally, she remarked, *"The bread is getting so stale that we hardly can eat it."*

The purser looked at them with a puzzled expression. Again he asked, *"Do you mean to tell me that you have been eating these stale sandwiches all the way from Ireland?"*

The young wife again explained their situation, that they could only afford the cheapest tickets and had nothing left over for food.

The purser stared at both for a few moments and finally said, *"Don't you know that your ticket also includes all the meals? In fact, you can eat as many meals each day as you so desire in any one of our several restaurants!"*

The lady stared at him for a moment and then finally said, *"Do you mean we have been eating these stale sandwiches all this time, when we could have had excellent meals each day, and as much as we desired?"*

"That's exactly what I mean," the purser said!

That describes most Christians!

We live so far beneath our spiritual privileges in Christ. We fight battles that long have already been won. We struggle with that which the Lord so long ago already defeated at the Cross of Calvary. Spiritually speaking, we eat stale sandwiches, whenever the Lord has set the table, and has set it so abundantly that it defies description; but yet, through Scriptural ignorance or unbelief, we refuse to sit down and partake of that which is so abundantly provided.

What a travesty!

The key is Christ and the Cross, as the key has always been Christ and the Cross!

As stated, there is a fight, but it is a *"good fight,"* simply because it is the *"right fight."*

If we are fighting the *"right fight,"* it's a fight that we definitely are going to win. In fact, there never has been a loser in this particular fight.

Let me say that again:

If one places one's faith in Christ and the Cross and maintains one's Faith in Christ and the Cross, the guarantee is sure. You are going to make it, and with flying colors!

Let me say it even once again:

There has never been a loser on this road of Faith in Christ and the Cross. In fact, there never will be a loser. Sadly, the other directions are freighted with losers on every hand. One cannot win by going in any other direction.

One can be saved and not subscribe to God's Prescribed Order of Victory; in other words, a Believer may live in a state of *"spiritual adultery."* But such a direction cannot know victory of any nature. As one of my associates has said, *"Many Believers are saved, but they are 'miserably saved.'"*

SELF-HELP STUDY NOTES

Chapter 5

Walking After The Flesh And Walking After The Spirit

CHAPTER FIVE

SELF-HELP STUDY NOTES

WALKING AFTER THE FLESH AND WALKING AFTER THE SPIRIT

When it comes to *"walking after the flesh"* or *"walking after the Spirit,"* most Believers don't really have a correct understanding of what Paul actually is saying here. Most don't know what *"the flesh"* actually means; while most all Believers know some things about the Holy Spirit, most simply do not know how to *"walk after the Spirit."* Consequently, they *"walk after the flesh,"* which means they are living in a state of *"spiritual adultery."*

Once again, please allow me to quote from THE EXPOSITOR'S STUDY BIBLE:

"There is therefore now no condemnation (guilt) *to them which are in Christ Jesus* (refers back to Romans 6:3-5 and our being baptized into His Death, which speaks of the Crucifixion), *who walk not after the flesh* (dependant on one's own personal strength and ability or great religious efforts in order to overcome sin), *but after the Spirit* (the Holy Spirit works exclusively within the legal confines of the Finished Work of Christ; our Faith in that Finished Work, i.e., *'the Cross,'* guarantees the help of the Holy Spirit, which guarantees Victory)*"* (Rom. 8:1).

WHAT DOES PAUL MEAN WHEN HE USES THE TERM *"FLESH"*?

In his fourteen Epistles (that is, if Paul wrote Hebrews, which I believe he did), he mentions the word *"flesh"* over ninety times. Approximately half of those times, he is referring to the word in a negative sense.

The Holy Spirit had him to use the word in order to explain a very important subject.

In the Greek, the word *"flesh"* is *"sarx,"* which means *"the body as opposed to the soul or spirit, with its frailties and passions."*

In simple terminology, when Paul uses the term in a negative sense, he is speaking of the ability, education, strength, power, self-will, and efforts of the human being, i.e., *"the flesh."* Within themselves, those things are not necessarily wrong; however, man, represented by *"the flesh,"* cannot effect his own Salvation, and neither can he effect proper life and living.

That's the reason Paul said, *"So then they who are in the flesh cannot please God"* (Rom. 8:8). This refers to the Believer attempting to live his Christian life by means other than Faith in Christ and the Cross.

He then said, *"For if you live after the flesh* (after your own strength and ability, which is outside of God's Prescribed Order) *you shall die* (you will not be able to live a victorious, Christian life)" (Rom. 8:13).

In brief, *"walking after the flesh"* refers to trying to live this life by any means other than Faith in Christ and the Cross. Actually, the Holy Spirit labels every effort made by man, irrespective as to what it is or how religious or zealous it might be, as *"the flesh,"* which means it is that which God cannot accept. And that's where the great struggle comes in.

That's why we at this Ministry are so opposed to all the latest fads, such as *"The Purpose Driven Life,"* etc. They are not preaching the Cross. They are not preaching the Cross at all! Therefore, what they are doing constitutes *"the flesh,"* which is totally unacceptable to God. As we've already said in this Volume, the unredeemed world has ever tried to fashion another god rather than the Lord of Glory, while the Church has tried to fashion another sacrifice other than the Cross of Christ.

Paul uses one of the terms, *"walk," "walked,"* or *"walking,"* over thirty times in his Epistles. The Greek word for *"walk"* is *"peripateo,"* which means *"the way that one deports oneself"* or *"the manner in which we live this life."*

When Paul used the term *"walking after the flesh,"* he was meaning that the Believer attempts to live for God by any means other than Faith in Christ and the Cross. In other words, he is functioning after schemes or plans made up by men, himself, or his Church, which are other than the Cross. That is what he means by *"walking after the flesh."* It is the same as living in a state of *"spiritual adultery."*

To help us understand it a little better, let us look at Christian disciplines.

CHRISTIAN DISCIPLINES

There are certain disciplines in which every good Christian will engage. I speak of prayer, Bible reading, witnessing, faithfulness to Church, financial support of the Work of God, etc. In other words, these all are things or disciplines in which every good Christian will engage himself.

Without a proper prayer life and without proper Bible Study, one cannot really have a relationship with Christ, which should be obvious. The other things, as well as many we have not named, fall into the same category. These disciplines, however, very easily can be turned into *"works,"* which constitute *"the flesh."*

Let me explain:

While a proper prayer life is an absolute necessity for the Child of God, still, such easily can be turned into works. For example, if we think that because we pray so much each day, or because we read so many Chapters in the Bible each day, this will give us victory over sin, we are woefully mistaken. They will not! These practices will result in our being blessed in many ways, and they will be profitable in many ways; but there will be no victory over sin gained by these directions.

Some, erroneously, will take the above statements and claim that we teach that Christians don't have to pray or don't have to study the Bible. Nothing could be further from the truth. What we are saying is that these tremendously valuable assets to Christian growth must not be turned into works.

When the Believer has his faith anchored firmly in Christ and the Cross, which is the only way of victory over sin, he will find that his prayer life, Bible Study, and every other Christian discipline will be of far more value than ever before.

SELF-HELP STUDY NOTES

WALKING AFTER THE SPIRIT

Most Christians think that *"walking after the Spirit,"* which refers, of course, to the Holy Spirit, is the carrying out of spiritual things. Once again, we go back to prayer, Bible reading, witnessing, etc. As valuable as those things are, that is not what Paul is speaking of when he speaks of *"walking after the Spirit."*

"Walking after the Spirit" is simply placing one's faith and trust exclusively in Christ and what Christ has done at the Cross. As we have stated in our explanation of Romans 8:2, this is the way the Holy Spirit works, which demands of us that the Cross of Christ ever be the Object of our Faith. Therefore, the answer to *"walking after the flesh"* and *"walking after the Spirit"* is very simple.

"Walking after the flesh" is placing one's faith in anything other than Christ and the Cross. *"Walking after the Spirit"* is one placing one's faith entirely in Christ and the Cross. It is just that simple!

EVERYTHING REVOLVES AROUND THE CROSS OF CHRIST

Paul said, *"We preach Christ Crucified"* (I Cor. 1:23). He said that for a purpose and a reason.

The Cross of Christ sums up the entirety of the New Covenant. In other words, everything revolves around the Cross.

Before the Cross, the Lord dealt with humanity, at least those who trusted Him, in a very complicated way. We speak of the Law of Moses and the Sacrificial System. And yet, before the Cross, people were saved exactly the same way as they are presently, with one exception.

Then, they were saved by looking forward to the Cross and what the Redeemer would do there, which was symbolized by the Sacrifices. Presently, people are saved by looking back to the Cross, to a price that already has been paid and to a victory that already has been won.

Before the Cross, the entirety of the world of Believers, ever how many there were, looked forward to a Prophetic Jesus, while presently, those who believe look back to an Historic Jesus. There has never been but one way of Salvation, and that is Jesus Christ and Him Crucified. And that one way is for all of mankind, both Jew and Gentile (Jn. 14:6).

So the idea that God has one way of Salvation for the Jews and another way for the Gentiles is blatantly false. As stated, there has never been but one way of Salvation and there never will be but one way of Salvation.

Because this is so very, very important, let us say it again:

Man is a sinner and he needs a Saviour. That Saviour, the only Saviour, is the Lord Jesus Christ. Salvation is afforded only by what the Saviour did at the Cross. One could say that the entirety of the Bible can be summed up in this oft-quoted Scripture:

"For God so loved the world, that He gave His Only Begotten Son, that whosoever believes in Him should not perish, but have Everlasting Life" (Jn. 3:16).

Chapter 6

Law Or Grace

CHAPTER SIX

SELF-HELP
STUDY NOTES

LAW OR GRACE

The following is quoted from THE EXPOSITOR'S STUDY BIBLE.

Paul said:

"For that which I do (the failure) *I allow not* (should have been translated, *'I understand not'*; these are not the words of an unsaved man, as some claim, but rather a Believer who is trying and failing)*: for what I would, that do I not* (refers to the obedience he wants to render to Christ, but rather fails. Why? As Paul explained, the Believer is married to Christ, but is being unfaithful to Christ by spiritually cohabiting with the Law, which frustrates the Grace of God; that means the Holy Spirit will not help such a person, which guarantees failure [Gal. 2:21])*; but what I hate, that do I* (this refers to sin in his life, which he doesn't want to do, and in fact hates, but finds himself unable to stop; unfortunately, due to the fact of not understanding the Cross as it refers to Sanctification, this is the plight of most modern Christians.)

"If then I do that which I would not (presents Paul doing something against his will; he doesn't want to do it, and is trying not to do it, whatever it might be, but finds himself doing it anyway)*, I consent unto the Law that it is good* (simply means that the Law of God is working as it is supposed to work; it defines sin, portraying the fact that the sin nature will rule in man's heart if not addressed properly).

"Now then it is no more I that do it (this has been misconstrued by many! It means, *'I may be failing, but it's not what I want to do.'* No true Christian wants to sin, because now the Divine Nature is in his life and it is supposed to rule, not the sin nature [II Pet. 1:4])*, but sin* (the sin nature) *that dwells in me* (despite the fact that some Preachers claim the sin nature is gone from the Christian, Paul here plainly says that the sin nature is still in the Christian; however, if our faith remains constant in the Cross, the sin nature will be dormant and cause us no problem; otherwise, it will cause great problems; while the sin nature *'dwells'* in us, it is not to *'rule'* in us)*"* (Rom. 7:15-17).

A MIXTURE OF LAW AND GRACE

Every Believer in the world is functioning either under Grace or Law, and more than likely under a mixture of both.

The mixture of both *"frustrates the Grace of God"* (Gal. 2:21), which greatly hinders the Holy Spirit from carrying out His Work within our hearts and lives. This state of *"Law and Grace mixture"* can be construed only as a position of *"spiritual adultery."* Considering that, one can well understand the position in which the Holy Spirit is placed within our lives.

The Believer is married to Christ, which means that we have the privilege of the Grace of God flowing uninterruptedly through our hearts and lives, which is superintended by the Holy Spirit, all made possible by the Cross, which supplies our every need; however, when the Believer resorts to Law of any nature, such constitutes *"spiritual adultery,"* because one is being unfaithful to Christ, i.e., *"our husband"* (II Cor. 11:1-2).

Chapter 7

What Is The Law?

CHAPTER SEVEN

SELF-HELP STUDY NOTES

WHAT IS THE LAW?

If most Christians were asked to define the Law, most instantly would think of the Law of Moses. While that definitely is Law, that really is not the Law that plagues the modern Christian.

Law definitely can be defined as the *"Law of Moses,"* which actually is the only true Law of its type that ever has existed, but it can also be defined as rules and regulations devised by religious men, or even the unredeemed, to help one reach God, or to better oneself in some way. Such laws, to be frank, are myriad, which means countless or innumerable. These are *"laws"* made up by Church Denominations, local Churches, Preachers, or even ourselves.

Many times these *"laws"* have some merit; in other words, within themselves, some of these laws are *"good."* As we already have written in this Volume, these laws deceive us exactly because they are *"good."*

Listen again to what Paul said about this matter. Once again, we quote from THE EXPOSITOR'S STUDY BIBLE:

"For sin (the sin nature), *taking occasion by the Commandment* (in no way blames the Commandment, but that the Commandment actually did agitate the sin nature and brought it to the fore, which it was designed to do), *deceived me* (Paul thought now that he had accepted Christ, by that mere fact alone, he certainly could obey the Lord in every respect; but he found he couldn't, and neither can you, at least in that fashion), *and by it slew me* (despite all of his efforts to live for the Lord by means of Law-keeping, he failed; and again, I say, so will you!)

"Wherefore the Law is Holy (points to the fact that it is God's Revelation of Himself; the problem is not in the Law of God, the problem is in us), *and the Commandment Holy, and just, and good* (the Law is like a mirror which shows man what he is, but contains no power to change him)*"* (Rom. 7:11-12).

Paul is speaking here of the Law of Moses. He is telling us that when we, as Christians, set out to try to keep Law, even the Law of Moses, and I speak of the moral part of that Law (the Ten Commandments), we are not going to successfully function in that capacity. Within himself, man, even redeemed man, cannot successfully keep the Law.

This is the most important: Jesus has already kept the Law for us. He did it totally, perfectly, and completely, all on our behalf.

So when a Believer places his faith exclusively in Christ and what

Christ has done for us at the Cross, then the moral Law will be perfectly kept without us even having to address it or even think about it. It is done by the Power of the Holy Spirit, Who Alone can carry out in our lives that which is demanded.

Having said that, however, the great problem Christians face, as stated, is laws made up by ourselves or by others. We think we can bring about Sanctification (or whatever) in our lives by keeping these laws.

We can't! Such always will end in failure. Again we state: Such direction is construed by the Lord as *"spiritual adultery."* It is a position that the Lord cannot accept, cannot abide, and definitely cannot bless. If a Believer stays in the position of *"Law,"* which *"frustrates the Grace of God,"* his spiritual situation steadily will deteriorate. In fact, such a one ultimately can lose his soul. I am not saying they definitely will, but I definitely am saying that they can, even as many have.

There are many today who once attempted to live for the Lord, who genuinely were Born-Again, but they have quit. If the truth be known, they have quit simply because, in their mind's eye, it just was too hard. The manner in which they were trying to live for God (which all of us, at one time or another, have tried) is too hard. The Lord cannot be served in that fashion.

GOD'S PRESCRIBED ORDER OF VICTORY

The Lord has but one way of victory, because only one way is needed. As we have said over and over, and as we will continue to say over and over, *"Christ is the Source of all things we receive from God, while the Cross is the Means by which these things are given to us."*

The Lord demands that we constantly and consistently exhibit faith in Christ and what He has done for us at the Cross. In other words, the Cross of Christ must ever be the Object of our Faith. That being done, the Holy Spirit, Who is God and Who can do anything, will then work mightily within our lives, developing His Fruit, ever drawing us closer to Christlikeness (Rom. 6:1-14; 8:1-2, 11; I Cor. 1:17-18, 21, 23; 2:2; Gal. 2:20-21; Gal., Chpt. 5; 6:14; Eph. 2:13-18; Col. 2:14-15).

If the Believer attempts to live for the Lord by any other means, no matter how good that other means might look or seem to be, failure will be the result. Invoking a play on words, it will be *"failure without fail."*

As we have stated elsewhere in this Volume, unredeemed man has ever tried to manufacture another god in the place of the Lord of Glory. The Church has ever tried to manufacture another sacrifice other than the Cross.

It is ever the Cross! The Cross! The Cross!

"Kneel at the Cross, Christ will meet you there,
"Come while He waits for you;
"List' to His Voice, leave with Him your care,
"And begin life anew.

"Kneel at the Cross, there is room for all
"Who would His Glory share.
"Bliss there awaits, harm can ne'er befall
"Those who are anchored there.

"Kneel at the Cross, give your idols up,
"Look unto realms above;
"Turn not away, to life's sparkling cup.
"Trust only in His Love."

CHORUS:

"Kneel at the Cross, leave every care;
"Kneel at the Cross, Jesus will meet you there."

SELF-HELP STUDY NOTES

SELF-HELP STUDY NOTES